Not what you'd expect

How the women's liberation
movement started

My personal experience of it

By Anne Wilensky

Published 2011 by Haiku Helen Press
Anne Pyne and Helen Kritzler

Written, edited, and published by Anne Pyne

All cartoons by Bill Pyne aka Billy Stampone

Drawing on front cover and cover design by
Helen Kritzler aka Haiku Helen

To order this book ask your local bookstore
Or go to www.createspace.com/3617012
Or order at any on-line bookseller

ISBN 978-0-9840976-3-0
0-98409776-3-5

Contact information: Willard Kraft
(520) 465-0999
5152 East 8th Street, Tucson, AZ 857

Printed in the United States of America

Women's liberation was an earthshaking experience for those of us who joined in its early days. I can only describe my own experience of it, and I have chosen to describe my first 5 months in it, from December '67 to May '68.

All my love, Anne

Thank you

For Bill, my wonderful husband who has made me so happy.

For Eddie, who got me to write this, and who has been my angel.

And for dear sweet wonderful Bob, a greater friend no girl could have.

You all asked me to write this and now I have. And I am glad I did.

All 3 of you told me it is *history* and because I was there and part of it I should say what happened because people don't know and they are interested.

I have no idea what others already know and if they are interested. All I know is that you guys don't know and you are interested. So I hope you find out what you want to know and you find it interesting.

I love all 3 of you now and forever

And thank all 3 of you for your faithful lifelong love encouragement support inspiration and friendship.

Your friend, Anne

All cartoons drawn by Bill Pyne, my husband

Bill draws our dog Skipper sleeping

Chapters

Preface

Hello

July 2008, Tucson, Arizona

Back in the fall when I was blogging with my Higher Self a lot, and She was talking about every topic under the sun, to my big surprise one of the topics She talked about was the Women's Liberation Movement. And I copy below some of the things she said about me back at that time. Because it is true. And following that is the 4 chapter story, written over this past week, I wrote about my experiences in Women's Liberation during its first year.

I joined it in December, 1967 when it was already in progress for 2 months, which means I missed the first 8-10 meetings, which is a lifetime in the birth of a new movement. Because of the huge burst of creativity which goes on at its inception.

And my story ends when I leave to go off to Europe for the summer in May, 1968. So this is about my 5 months at Women's Liberation, the first year of its existence.

Communicated from my Higher Self

The truth is Anne never really understood women's liberation, altho she was direct beneficiary of it. In other words women's liberation instantly liberated her. If I were to confide where Anne's mind was before women's liberation, it would be a total embarrassment to her.

She completely believed in being feminine, which was some disastrous, awful, prettily-wrapped version of being second class citizen in all ways.

Her mind was awash with firm beliefs only a very young teenager, a boy-crazy young teenager, could ever believe. She had completely romanticized the disempowerment of women.

A poor pathetic oppressed creature had walked into her

first women's liberation movement meeting with no idea why she was there. "Why am I at a meeting of all women! All I want to do is find a boyfriend. And women are not oppressed, we have the vote," she thought, "this is all ridiculous."

And instantly women's liberation liberated her. It happened at that first meeting and kept right on going. Every false idea in her mind was replaced by truth.

And by the time she stopped showing up at meetings a year later, she was liberated, as liberated as she would get. Altho she still has a long way to go to understand men still have the power in the world, women don't, and why it is absolutely necessary power be shared between the sexes.

Other than consciousness raising, she had nothing to offer women's liberation, she could only receive. So her story is how the women's liberation movement liberated her.

By Anne

Everything my Higher Self says here is true, but I still had a glorious time being part of Women's Liberation during its first two years.

I had not intended to write about women's liberation, even tho I promised Eddie Kritzler I would. And I kind of got sucked into it in the first chapter. I kept thinking I would go back to saying how I had decided not to write about it. But I kept on going.

That chapter is short and I am sorry I did not give it my all, because that is where the heart is. The love, and the love which melted my heart.

By the next morning and the morning after that, I was into it. I did try to write it to the best of my ability. And now that I did it, I am glad I did. And I owe it all to Eddie and to Bob Carneiro.

Love, Anne

Anne writes this because Bob and Eddie ask her to

At the 7/11

Women's liberation was an awakening for me

Wake up Anne! It's 1967, the women's liberation movement has started

My First Women's Liberation Meeting

written July 10, 2008, early morning Tucson, AZ

Well it is a soft and dreamy morning. Monsoon weather is a trip. It sprinkled while we were swimming yesterday at noon and by 1 pm when the children arrived, it had even turned into real rain. The little girls were all at the end of pool by the steps chanting "Rain rain go away! Come again another day!"

But there was no thunder storm yesterday, little

Beanie (our dog) got a reprieve. He was finally able to enjoy his food and have two helpings and be relaxed and happy all day. It may have sprinkled on and off all day yesterday because this morning is so soft, not misty exactly, but cloudy and warm soft air. Like a morning in the tropics, but not a desert weather, it feels tropical instead.

I sent my story *My mom, Me, and my Higher Self*, which I had written 2 days ago but did not finish fixing typos till yesterday morning, to Eddie and to Bob along with my girlfriends.

Eddie was the first one to respond. His response was "why don't you write about the start of women's liberation, that is what everyone wants to hear about."

Which is what Bob had been writing to me all along. I just giggled at Eddie's email at first, because Eddie has flair for writing emails which blow my mind and make me burst into giggles even tho they are only 3 sentences.

But when I wrote back saying "you are sweet to encourage me in my writing," he wrote back "this is not an answer, will you do it or not."

He meant it apparently, he really meant I should write the story of the start of women's liberation. And Eddie does have talent for getting me to do what he wants me to do. So

I gave it long hard thought and decided I will.

And I wrote back "OK, I will give it a whirl, you succeeded in convincing me to do it."

And he emailed "**hooray**" in huge big block bold letters.

And so I did start to think about how to start off the story. Once a story is started it is easy as pie just to keep going, it all flows naturally.

And I realized I did have an idea how to start it off. I remembered I was walking with Iris on East 6th Street. I had an apartment there that year, and I knew Iris from City College. We hadn't been friends in college but we had brief two week friendship this year after college (1967).

When I was walking with her on 6th Street and I said to her "there is this thing happening now called women's liberation, do you think women need to be liberated?"

And she thought about it and said "no."

And I said "neither do I."

But wherever I went those days— I was in the left-wing radical '60s world back then, but because I was in the East Village they were all hippies too— and whatever I went to, there would be some girl talking about going to the women's liberation meeting that Thursday.

And so that Thursday I tried to find it. I didn't succeed,

but the following Thursday I did. I showed up. And in between I began to think about all the possible ways women could need to be liberated. I was trying to get my mind to accept this new idea, to see why it could be good thing.

And by the time I did find the meeting the following Thursday, I was completely open-minded on the topic and curious. The meeting was at Anne Koedt's apartment, above the Jewish appetizing store, and the back room must have been big.

She must have had big apartment, because I walked all thru her apartment and arrived in back room where there were about 50 women it seemed to me.

On the way to her back bedroom I passed her boyfriend Javier and his friend in the kitchen. They were quietly talking and when I said "where is the meeting?" they pointed.

And of course what struck me when I first arrived— the meeting was already in sway— is what struck everyone back then at their first meeting, how intelligent each of the women were.

I had no idea women were so intelligent. And I had been to gazillion radical meetings of men, and I had never noticed one intelligent word spoken. They would all just get very wild and say very wild things.

I was used to that was how meetings were, the men were in charge and would be wild and say wild things, and then it was over. It was always totally meaningless. But I guess I had a good time anyway or I wouldn't have gone, or I believed this is how you make a revolution, and I was a revolutionary back then.

The meeting of the women for women's liberation was the opposite. They were all calm, sitting on the floor, there was no leader. Most of the women did talk, and each one was extraordinarily intelligent. As Linda Feldman said about going to her first meeting, "I felt like I had arrived on the moon."

And naturally I fell in love with it instantly and was totally liberated, because what was outstanding and clear, was we were doing this for all women. We were determined to liberate all women, ourselves and all the women in the world.

It was the first liberation group I had ever belonged to which was not for liberating someone else, but for liberating me.

And the idea that this was for ourselves and all women,

meant that for the very first time in my life I did not see myself in competition with every other woman. The world of jealousy envy competition dropped out, because we united for all women. We were united with all women.

It was an expression of love for all women instead of seeing each and every one as a competitor. So instead of being totally alone and isolated and in competition with every other woman, I was now joined with all women for our mutual happiness. I saw them as a sister instead of a competitor.

It was freedom from hate, jealousy, envy, competition. I could simply love all the women in the room and by extension all women. And what can be more freeing than to be liberated from hate, jealousy, envy, competition, to simple love.

I trusted them and I loved them, they trusted me and loved me. And the love and trust bloomed. It was a beautiful thing, and it all happened in 15 minutes of the first meeting.

It was the first time I had been in a roomful of women where we weren't all in competition with each other, but loved each other and were unified instead.

And I remember being at another meeting a few months later, when Anne Koedt read her list. It must have been the stages of womanhood and how we will liberate women at all stages. And I think my eyes teared up when she got to 12 year old girls, and I had tenderness of heart when she got to end, at old women.

I was just so touched that we cared about 12 year old girls. I thought "no one ever has cared about 12 year old girls, they have always been seen as totally unimportant, as 'don't matter.'" And of course old women, when you are 22 years old, seemed irrelevant from the eyes of the world too. Who in the world cared about 12 year old girls and old women except us! We were for 12 year old girls and old women. To us they mattered more than the world.

And at that moment I fell totally in love with women's liberation. I had always been in love with it, but this was kind of the apotheosis for me. My heart totally melted. I loved Anne Koedt, I loved everyone in my group. And most of all I loved the movement I was part of. The movement which would liberate 12 year old girls and old women. We were for them when no one else was.

More on that first meeting and other early meetings

Of course your first women's liberation meeting is a sea of women. Even tho Anne Koedt's apartment seemed to be like a railroad flat, like all the tenements in the East Village, because it was on Second Avenue, it was structured all differently. That back room was incredibly wide.

Where the door opened up seemed to be the New York women, sitting all the way to end on the side in a big clump together. All the pretty brunette New York women, with that look of New York all over them.

And everyone in the room seemed to be in their early twenties. This was a true '60s thing.

The rest of the room seemed to be a big circle, I mean women sitting in a big circle. And there was a woman who was chairman of the meeting. I discovered the meetings were held in a different girl's house each week and the chairman was different each week and the chairman was never the girl whose house it was in.

The idea of a different chairman each week, was the idea that women never got to be leaders, so we would rotate chairmen and each would get a chance to be leader.

This did not last very long because it seems to me the next meeting I went to— a lot happened between this meeting and the next one. For one thing women's liberation had done a major action in Washington DC, the Jeanette Rankin Brigade. I didn't go to it.

But between that event, which took place in January— the meeting I had gone to was in December— I guess instead of meetings they had prepared for that event.

In any case Carol Hanisch, one of the women, worked for SCEF on 4th Avenue, and she offered the SCEF office as place to have our meetings. So we always met there, and there was no chairman at all.

At the meeting I went to, my first meeting, the chairman was a girl named Barbara I think. I didn't notice anything wrong with how she chaired the meeting, but what did I know! It was my first meeting.

But she must have done something wrong, because shortly into the meeting there were complaints she was acting like a PTA committee-woman chairman.

I still don't know what she did wrong. But whatever she

was doing was against the spirit of what women's liberation was.

The women spoke up boldly and clearly and directly. That was a shock. I was used to whisper campaigns behind someone's back, not open honest direct assertion.

And I found it interesting and refreshing that they didn't want to put up with a bossy committee chairman.

I was so used to the way the world worked— was that the awful was always given pride of place, that the awful was deemed good, and what is natural and freeing is deemed bad.

But that is not how women's liberation worked, the awful was deemed awful. So everyone spoke up, and that was it. For the rest of the meeting there was no chairman. I guess the job was just taken away from her.

I was just interested that a whole type of interaction had gone on that I had never seen before. They didn't act like women had always acted, they were bold, direct, honest, and for freedom.

I don't remember the early discussion very well. I guess it was all plans for their big action in Washington. And most of the women in that big circle who did most of the talking did not seem to be New Yorkers.

I remember a tall blond from Texas who talked a lot.

One girl had long thick braids, glasses, brown hair, brown eyes, and was wearing brown corduroy pants. She reminded me so much of my best friend when I was 4 years old, Debbie Bernstein, that I instantly loved her. Also I noticed she was the only one eating the cookies.

She looked so familiar to me, that instant the meeting was over, I went over to her and said "where do I know you from?"

But it turned out she had grown up in St Louis and been in Chicago all this time. We both knew Amy Kesselman in common, but that did not explain why she looked so familiar to me. But I guess you could say I loved her. I even invited her back to my apartment when meeting was over so we could get to know each other.

I guess when I realized how much I loved women's liberation at that first meeting, it seemed important to me to find out how we were oppressed as women. I still had no idea. So I asked. I said "I am new at this and I have no idea, can you give me some examples."

It seems to me by now the whole big New York contingent in the corner had left. Because when we went around in a circle saying our own experiences, it was just the same people who had been in that big circle.

I guess the girl Barbara who had been chairman had left in a huff because she has been removed as chairman.

I don't remember what everyone said as we talked about our experiences as we sat in circle, but the girl with red hair (Carol Hanisch) said she grew up on a farm in Iowa, and the women did all the farm chores same as men, but in addition they did all the women's work, the cooking and the cleaning, etc, and that isn't fair.

She thought work should be divided equally. And this made perfect sense to me. Why not!

I don't remember what else was said because I got so excited thinking what I would say when it was my turn to talk.

And then the meeting was over. That was when I went over to that dark-haired girl in braids who reminded me so much of Debbie Bernstein, and we talked, and I invited her back to my apartment.

And then we talked half the night. It turned out she was an artist, a painter, and she had such strong clear ideas about everything.

She said "In art school there were girls who made their own clothes and did all kinds of other things, but they never became good artists because they spread themselves too thin."

And she said "The best artist in art school said 'there is no such thing as talent.'"

And I learned that the reason she had started women's liberation was because the art world doesn't give women a chance, and she wants to be a recognized artist.

I had never met anyone before with ambition, or an artist, or someone who had absolutely clear strong original ideas on everything. My idea of our spending an evening getting to know each other had been far chummier and more girly.

That it would be a normal friendship, and we would be equals. After all from my point of view she didn't know how to dress or do her hair, or do anything to be sexy and beautiful. My own friends were all beautiful and glamorous, this was a big departure for me.

But I had found her irresistible at the meeting, she reminded me so much of Debbie Bernstein who I had loved loved loved when I was 4 years old.

But my idea that she would be even more fun than my glamorous beautiful friends turned out not to be true. It wasn't what I would call a chummy evening at all.

I could not say one word, because all her ideas were so strong, so clear, so thought out, so original and so serious. How the world really worked.

And I had no ideas.

I wound up extremely impressed with her, which was not what I anticipated when I wanted to be best friends with her.

It was probably 3 am now, so I said "why don't you sleep over."

And she said "I never feel like myself unless I wake up in my own bed," and so she left.

I was used to girls finding a sleepover date fun, I always did, but she was a breed of another color. She had focus and she didn't want to lose her focus.

And so this is the first girl I became friends with in women's liberation, and she was awesome, her name was Shulie.

The next meeting I went to was at the SCEF office. It was a huge big room and there were not so many of us, and there was no chairman.

The discussion was random, but it seemed earthshaking to me. Even tho we were all so young, some women were married and had little ones. There was a lot of discussion about housework. Why should it be the woman's job to do it all, why not share it?

This was revolutionary idea to me, but I went for it!

And then somehow the conversation turned to, why can't the husband stay home with the kids if you have to go to a job interview or something important?

And Jennifer Gardiner, she was one of the young mothers, said "what if you just want to go to the movies?"

I was shocked! This was such a new concept. But there was something totally liberating in it.

Then Shulie said something about "how women are always shunted into the helping professions."

And of course this totally blew my mind.

I had been brought up by my father who had explained to me because I am a girl I have two choices, I can be a secretary or go into the helping professions. And he felt the helping professions would be more rewarding choice for me.

I was completely idealistic about the helping professions. My dad was a school teacher, my mom was a nurse, everyone in my family was in the helping professions, it was considered noble work.

It had never occurred to me to want to do anything else. I had always assumed I would be a school teacher, altho I was working as social worker my first year in women's liberation.

What Shulie said shocked me down to my underpants. Because her idea was that we could dream higher and dream bigger, even if I didn't know exactly what that dream was. But certainly it implied we could be anything.

And then it seemed the next thing which happened at the meeting, is Shulie complained about it. She said "This is like a slumber party in boarding school! We should be taking action!"

I guess she found the discussion valueless, she wanted action! But I liked the discussion, I was learning from it. But of course I found it thrilling when she dismissed it all as slumber party in boarding school and wanted action instead.

I guess by the end of that second meeting it was clear to me that Shulie was really the leader of this leaderless movement, because she had the clear vision of what we would accomplish and how we would accomplish it.

And it does seem as if there was some meeting in my own apartment, I don't know why, maybe just ten of us, where everyone got mad at Shulie and said "You think you are the only one who wants this to be a serious movement and accomplish women's liberation for all. But I see this as a movement which will sweep the country and then sweep the world." They all said this.

And I secretly thought "good luck!" I had been in revolutionary groups my whole life and they never accomplished anything. No revolution ever happened! I knew from experience nothing ever happens! Nothing is ever accomplished!

I thought "they sure are dreamers, 10 women sitting around a little tenement apartment in the East Village, thinking they will accomplish a world-wide movement!"

I didn't say it of course, but it was what I thought.

And boy how wrong I was!

I simply had no understanding of this movement I was part of.

I think it was at that meeting in my apartment when Kathie and Carol unveiled the new slogans they had come up with for our movement. *Sisterhood is powerful* and *The personal is political.*

And because Kathie had noticed, when we went around in a circle at that first meeting I had been to, talking about our own experiences, ways we had been oppressed as women, she named that experience *consciousness raising*, it raised our awareness of our own oppression.

And based on it Carol came up with the slogan *The personal is political.*

The personal is political is very interesting. There were always huge fights when it was suggested we could learn more about something by going around in a circle and saying our own personal experiences in this.

Shulie was always against it, she definitely thought it was "slumber party at boarding school" waste of time. But Kathie was totally into it, she thought it raised our consciousness, and I would line up with Kathie on this.

Whenever a new girl would arrive at our meeting, and we would decide to do consciousness-raising, the new girl would protest. "I heard you do this, but how is this revolutionary! How is this making a revolutionary movement and liberating anyone! This is just group therapy!"

But when we would do it and include the new girl, she would become converted instantly.

I guess the first crisis, or split, occurred after I had been going to meetings for a few months.

The Free University had started up on 14th Street, a meeting place for radicals. Women's liberation had had a thing there, which is how many women in New York found out about it. Many radical women, not just from the East Village, but from all over New York City. And they all wanted to go to a meeting.

For some reason Ros, who had started to come to our meetings, wasn't able to leave her apartment. She had toddler son and maybe her husband was away. So she said "let's have the meeting at my apartment," she had a big apartment. And instead of it being 14 women, it was jammed with all these new women.

And Florika arrived! This was thrilling! She had a middle European accent and she looked like a ravishing gypsy. Her beauty and romantic looks were flooring. Plus her dramatic way of talking! There could have been a great movie actress in our midst.

What she actually said, was not where we were at anymore. It was long diatribes about Marxist Leninism and how we should be like that. But who cared what she said! It was how she said it and how she looked!

She was so thrilling! And I knew her exhorting us to be

devoted Marxist Leninists would have zero effect. I had come out of that background and so had many of the others there, or some of the others anyway.

And this was just a completely different path and it was the right path and we all knew it. But we all fell in love with Florika and wanted her in our group.

But the reverse happened. There was a split, half the group decided to form their own group. I don't know what they didn't like about our group, what they wanted which was not happening. It was called *the Wednesday night group* because they met on Wednesday evenings.

And then they still came to our big Thursday evenings group, but they acted differently. They acted like a clique, and were always either touching each other or whispering to each other. And we all felt excluded because we were not invited to join the Wednesday night group. And this is the group Florika joined. She never came back to one of our meetings.

And I guess it must have been at a meeting at Ros's apartment— either there were two meetings there, or so much happened at one. No! it had to be a separate meeting— that a lot of fights broke out.

The first fight I didn't get at all, it must have been very very early in my going to women's liberation meetings. Apparently our group had been started by Pam and Shulie.

Maybe they had come from Chicago to New York together and started it here. The fight was about something called, it seems to me now "the black analogy." I guess Pam wanted our group to mirror the direction of the civil rights groups in the South, and Shulie wanted us to set our own direction. I don't know?

I just know a huge fight broke out about this, and when it was over, Pam had lost. She left and never came back. And a few days later, when I was at Free University, I heard her talking about it to her friends, "I made that group and now I will break it."

I guess she was mad. She didn't recognize me even tho I was in the same room. I was such a nobody.

The next fight which broke out was between Kathie and Peggy. Peggy was the tall blond Texan who talked a lot, and Kathie was very petite blond from Long Island who looked like Mia Farrow.

Peggy looked like twice her size. And those two did most of the talking at the meetings. Shulie actually said very little at meetings and Carol was not a big talker either.

I liked to talk.

Apparently Kathie was talking and I guess Peggy didn't like what she was saying, because Peggy kept saying "shut up!" And Kathie refused to shut up. And finally big tall Peggy just sat behind her and put her hands on Kathie's mouth. And Kathie was furious!

After I moved to Tucson, I was on the phone once with Carol, she was living in upstate New York now, and I recalled that incident. I said "what did we do after it happened?"

And she said "we had a big discussion about it."

Which made me smile fondly. Women's liberation was still in such a healthy phase then, that that is exactly what we would do, have big discussion about it. Everything back then was so upfront and direct, and out in the open and clear and cleansing.

I guess the fight was over "let the quiet women talk." This is something we would fight about a lot. Someone would say "some people here do all the talking, and they should shut up and let the quiet women talk."

Instantly that was said, I would shut up and feel guilty, because I was one of the big talkers. But Kathie would not be intimidated, she would just go right on talking. And I guess that is why Peggy put her hands over her mouth.

And so the discussion afterwards was about "let the quiet women talk." And Judy Duffet said, "I am a quiet woman and I don't want to be made to talk."

And that ended it! The big talkers were allowed to talk as much as they wanted after that, which was nice for me, I liked to talk.

I don't know if Peggy came back to another meeting after that. I guess she just went to the Wednesday night meetings.

Sex and More on Meetings

I am writing about the early days of women's liberation because both Bob and Eddie asked me to, they want to read it, or they think others will want to read it, or both. And I can't say no to either Bob or Eddie, I adore both of them. Altho I wonder if I would be writing it if both hadn't asked me, as it was the last thing I ever planned to write about.

I'm not sure what else there is to write about. I joined in December (1967) it had probably been going for two months at that point, and someone else will have to write about its glorious inception, since I was not there for that.

Some things had already been worked out by the time I arrived. We would have no leaders so every woman would get an experience in leadership.

And when we did actions which got the attention of the press, altho this came later, the decision had been taken way back before I arrived that any woman would talk to the press.

The idea behind this was to open experiences to women we never had. It's a man's world after all (not that we weren't all about changing that). In fact it made women's liberation totally democratic, we were all equals.

One big idea which emerged with consciousness-raising (going around in a circle and each saying our own personal experience in whatever area we were talking about) is the idea that women are the experts on women, not the men authorities.

Like every new revolutionary idea, after it is realized, it seems absolutely natural and normal and sensible and obvious, anything else seems insane. But that is what a revolution is, the move from insanity to sanity.

And like everything else in the '60s, women's liberation was turning upside down what our experience of the world had been in the '50s, the beliefs we had all grown up on— the world which had been handed to us, and which some of us subscribed to and some of us didn't.

I mean women's liberation would never have happened if some didn't subscribe to those beliefs, because it was all about overturning those beliefs, and substituting them with new ones. But I am guessing most subscribed to the old beliefs, at least I did, else why was it so revolutionary! I mean such a revolution in consciousness.

And of course right now it seems like a lot of chutzpah for male authorities to be the experts on women. But that was how it was before women's liberation, and that is what women's liberation overthrew.

We decided women are the experts on women. And we would find out what women were like by going around in a circle and saying our own experiences. Then we would have a solid base to work from. Which is true.

Altho it was liberating to the mind to decide everything male experts had said about women (what we were like and what we should be like) was hogwash. And just throw it all out, and have clean slate—

Naturally the nitty gritty was sex. We were all young. Young marrieds. Or had lived with boyfriends. Were living with boyfriends. Or looking for a boyfriend. And if we were looking for a boyfriend we were sleeping around. It was the '60s and that is what girls did then.

Now Sigmund Freud (the expert of all experts, the authority figure of all authority figures) had ordained that women could have two types of orgasm, clitoral and vaginal. God only knows now how he came up with this!

As far as I know Sigmund Freud is a guy, not a gal, how

he could decide he was expert on women's sexuality beats me! The only thing he can be expert on is men's sexuality.

But that didn't stop him from ordaining on women's sexuality. But he didn't stop at saying there were two kinds of orgasms we could have, he claimed that one meant we were arrested at very immature level, the clitoral orgasm, and vaginal orgasm meant we were a real woman. Wow!

And god help us, we all believed it. The problem is no one had ever had a vaginal orgasm. But since this was a deep dark secret that no woman confided to each other or to anyone, because it means "we were not a real woman."

What happened were two things. Each woman carried around a sense of lack, as if she were lacking. And second of all the solution of faking orgasm came up. When you were sleeping around, the boys expected you to have an orgasm when you had sex with them.

And of course faking orgasm is a big drag!

I really don't know how it happened. My own memory says it all happened in Ratner's restaurant after I got back from Europe that first summer. But that must be impossible, because when Shulie and Anne Koedt put out that little booklet, *Notes of the First Year*, with short articles about things we had learned in our first year, Anne Koedt did write the article about orgasm.

So it must have been in the Spring. It may have been a Sunday morning, else why were we all at Ratner's having breakfast together (and not at work).

There was Anne K, there was me, and there were two other girls from our group. I have vague memory of what they looked like, one was petite brunette, pretty, who wore a scarf on her head a lot. I don't remember the other one, and there even could be a third one.

But it is perfect illustration that women's liberation was never about a handful of women whose names got remembered, but was about a sea of women who floated in and out of meetings, or even were just around at the time.

God only knows why we were talking about orgasms at breakfast at Ratner's. But naturally sex is a big topic when you are young and it is the '60s, it was our life.

And we sat there, all 4 of us, and each of us admitted we never had vaginal orgasm. Something we had never admitted to anyone else in our life, not even to our very closest girlfriends. It could only take place in the context of women's liberation.

And that is the extraordinary thing about women's liberation, in fact that is it in a nutshell. It allowed reality to come forth, and nothing else did.

And that is the kind of mind we had back then in women's liberation. Once we discovered that all 4 of us had never had a vaginal orgasm, it took nothing for us to leap to the conclusion that vaginal orgasm does not exist, all there is, is clitoral orgasm, which we all did have.

And we sat there so freed and liberated. Because of course it meant we were all normal women, we were fine as we were. And not totally lacking as Sigmund Freud had proclaimed us to be. Like everything having to do with liberation, it happens in an instant.

By the time we finished drinking our coffee at Ratner's, I knew I would never fake another orgasm again. LOL I was totally freed from faking orgasms! That was a relief!

Plus I knew I was fine. Plus it left me free to explore my own sexuality wherever it led me. And I guess Anne Koedt went right upstairs and wrote that article *The Myth of the Vaginal Orgasm* which came out in **Notes from the First Year.**

Our conversation must have been in May right before I left for Europe because I don't remember talking about it at a meeting before I left for Europe. But a month later when Shulie arrived in France herself, to bring copies of **Notes** *from the First Year* to give to Simone de Beauvoir (she and Anne together tried to bring it to her, but the concierge would not let them in)— Anne K's article was already in there.

And I will say when I was briefly in group therapy a few years later, the therapist, Nancy Edwards, brought out Anne's article, it was now in some other format, to hand to a man in the group.

Can you believe that! Can you believe that every female practicing psychotherapist had also bought Freud's line hook, line, and sinker, and it took women's liberation to liberate the whole psychology establishment on that!

LOL I wonder where Freud came up with such a cockamamie idea to begin with! He liked to smoke coke, and maybe the idea came to him that way. It was one of the stoned ideas he had. Some were very creative and true, I give him a lot of credit. That dreams are wish fulfillment, is beyond brilliant, and lies at the heart of everything. He probably came up with that on coke.

But women's sexuality, I am not sure coke is the best way to learn about that. He must have been a terrible lover, and did not know how to bring any pleasure to his wife, to have arrived at an understanding of women's sexuality which had zero understanding in it.

And what makes it so dangerous, because the whole psychology establishment promulgated it, is it was guaranteed to ruin the sex life of every other man and woman.

I mean how could it be a good thing that every woman would feel like a failure as a woman because there was some kind of orgasm, "the real kind" according to Freud, that she was not having. And where did it leave the guy!

Either she had to fake it, so he thought he had "accomplished it" or he had to think he was unable to give her the "real orgasm."

I am just saying it was a big burden Freud placed on everyone just because he did not have a good sex life with his wife himself.

And of course that ended on the spot in Ratner's restaurant that morning. Because it spread thru women's liberation like wildfire. The following year there was brief period when it was all we talked about. And at the big Chicago conference the following Thanksgiving, where women from all over the country came, it was topic A. Everyone talked about their sex life, it got a lot of play.

There is no question women's liberation liberated

women sexually, which is a good thing. But a few years before I left New York for Tucson when Leslie was visiting, she said "Have you heard about the G spot?"

Apparently this is some spot that no one can ever find, but it is the spot of "real sex." Leslie was never in women's liberation so maybe she didn't understand.

"Leslie!" I said, "how can you fall for this! After all we went thru to liberate women sexually! Why would you fall for this and start this thing all over again! That there is something wrong with you because you haven't experienced your G spot."

Leslie fell for it hook, line, and sinker, but I decided not to fall for it at all. It had taken so much to liberate ourselves from the malarkey in the first place, why should I buy into it now.

And of course it was huge relief to stop faking orgasm with the guys I was sleeping around with. I never did fake another orgasm after that conversation in Ratner's.

And I want to say again, every mind in women's liberation was valuable and key. Here at Ratner's were two girls who showed up at the meetings but I have no idea their names now. I don't remember ever having private conversation with them. And yet none of this could have happened without them.

There were millions of anonymous women in women's liberation, and yet each of their minds played key part. I don't know anything about other movements, but this was a genuine grassroots movement. Every woman's mind was needed. It could not have happened without them.

Back to the Meetings at the SCEF office that first year

The thing I remember about my second meeting at the SCEF office altho it could have been my third. It was still early, before Ros arrived— it must have still been that original core group which had been at Anne Koedt's apartment when I first showed up. Is that unaccountably they all voted to throw Shulie out of the group.

This seemed like an insane choice to me. And I have no idea why they wanted it. And where was Anne K! There was no way she would go along with it!

Maybe there was a vote, that had to be it, and we who voted to keep Shulie in were outnumbered.

But I didn't care about any vote! I knew she was the leader. I knew she gave direction. I knew she had the vision. I wasn't going to let her be thrown out of our group!

And I didn't!

I don't know why they wanted to throw her out. I guess because she had a problem of rubbing people the wrong way. She had a problem letting others feel equal to her. Which affected our personal friendship, inevitably my ego acted up and I didn't have the sense to control it.

But I could care less about it at women's liberation meetings, which were for women's liberation.

They were all beautiful meetings those first meetings that first year. Altho oddly enough, after every meeting, everyone said what a bad meeting it was.

Sometimes older women joined, which was nice. Women's liberation erased the age barrier I noticed. Before that I would have thought an older woman had zero interest in me, that I didn't exist for her. But women's liberation just made us all equal as women and vitally interested in each other as women for women.

And two little lesbians joined, which thrilled us. We felt we were succeeding in our goal, which was to include every woman in women's liberation.

And then it came time for the end-of-the-year party. I was leaving for Europe the next week. And a young married woman suggested "Did anyone here consider we might not invite men to the party?"

And Shulie instantly said "What's a party without men!"
And I agreed.

Shulie and I were looking for boyfriends, and parties is
one of the places you hoped to meet one. But I guess the
young married women thought the party wouldn't be fun
for them if they had to bring their husband, and some girls
were living with their boyfriends too.

In any case a vote was taken, and the vote was not to
invite men to the party. So neither Shulie nor I went. She
came over to my apartment where I packed up for leaving
for Europe the next day.

I know Bob wants to hear about who the women were in
our group and what they were like, so maybe tomorrow I
will tell about that. Except for Shulie and maybe Kathie
(who became leaders) we were such ordinary regular nice
women. The only thing we had which was at all unusual
was we all had passion for freedom, which is why I was a
hippy back then too. And we were all eccentric, I guess I'd
have to say that too.

I guess I should say something about the advent of Ellen
Willis joining. Ellen liked to theorize, which a lot of
fun. I guess we all liked to theorize with her. Whether these
theories added up to anything, I don't know. But it was

something we all enjoyed doing together at the meetings.

I know I didn't describe any of the actions we did, or the women in my group. All that is here is my first 5 months in women's liberation, before I left for Europe for the summer. As I said, other than Shulie and Kathie (Shulie was the leader while I was there, Kathie became a leader after I left women's liberation) the women in my group were normal friendly kind gentle helpful beings. And fun loving. Not all were so young in age. But all had young happy spirit, and I loved them all very much. We had a great time.

Part 2

The David Susskind Show

We all go out to a restaurant together after the meetings

The David Susskind Show

I had missed The Miss America protest. It took place in September after I got back from Europe and was living in a different apartment.

The girl I had sublet to, Marion's sister (I had met Marion in women's lib) — her sister had let an older woman stay in the apartment, then her sister left it, then the older woman left it. And when I returned to New York City I no longer had an apartment.

So I found a new one on First Avenue. It was a much nicer apartment than the one I had had, which was not nice at all. And in fact I stayed in that First Avenue apartment till Bill and I and our dog moved to Tucson.

Back then I was outraged that Marion's sister had just given away my apt. and I had no apt. to return to, plus all my stuff was gone. But the Universe has its own way of arranging a change for the better be made. And it was better I move into the other apartment. It was a little prettier and a little roomier and the windows looked out on trees in backyard.

I had not yet learned how to clean my house tho. I kept saying I should do it, and thought I should do it, but I never did. I was working full-time and when the weekends arrived I just wanted to play. I never wanted to clean my house and I didn't know how. But it was what I always planned to do on the week-end.

So the day of the Miss America protest in Atlantic City, I walked to Union Square, where everyone gathered to get on the bus to Atlantic City. But I decided I wouldn't go, I would stay home and clean my house instead.

Of course I wound up not cleaning my house. It wasn't till the Spring of that year that I finally figured out how to clean my house, and cleaned it from top to toe, and had that joy of pretty, clean house. It was just a huge big mess the first 4 months I lived there.

The Miss America protest was huge. I missed out on a major event. And it was how the media discovered women's liberation, since they were all there covering the Miss America Contest.

Women's liberation became "women's lib." And because Carol had the "garbage can of oppression" there for women to throw in their bras and girdles, "women's libbers" were "bra burners."

When I had gone out with my family and relatives for dinner in China Town and mentioned I was a member of the women's liberation movement, everyone at the table had a big laugh about it. They thought it was hysterically funny that there was such a thing as the women's liberation movement, and that Annie was in it.

And I guess so did *The New York Daily News*, which broke the news about the women's liberation movement the day after the Miss America contest. They thought we were a hysterically funny movement.

"Women's libbers burn bras at Miss America Contest," is how the women's liberation movement was announced to the world.

Women's liberation was thrilled with the media attention. "Now everyone will know about women's liberation" Kathie said at the next meeting.

Shulie was still in Europe. She missed The Miss America protest and the meeting which followed. Kathie claimed that *The New York Daily News* was our best friend, they are the first ones who covered us. At that time all anyone cared about was getting out the word about women's liberation, so that all women would join the women's liberation movement.

We wanted a mass movement, and Kathie was correct, mass media was the way to spread the word. She is right *The New York Daily News* did us a huge favor.

And because of it, our meetings became gigantic. Even 16 year old girls arrived, who during consciousness raising sessions (which now took up whole meeting, there were so many of us) told about how they had been one of the little girls dragged kicking and screaming from the Beatles concerts, they had not been able to control themselves and had rushed the stage. Their life had been the Beatles.

And journalists showed up. They were a little older than us, and sat together and had different atmosphere. We didn't know they were journalists, they just participated like everyone else, and got swept up into it too.

It was how they joined women's liberation. I only found out much later that they had been sent by their editors to "find out what these chicks are up to."

And that is why we got an invitation to appear on the *David Susskind Show*. Apparently David Susskind had invited a spokesman from our group, and one from NOW, and two other women, to be the panel on his show to talk about women's liberation.

Altho I didn't know that when we all walked over to his studio in the East 30s. All we knew is we would be on, that women's liberation would be on TV.

We were so thrilled. It was our chance to communicate to all women. This was a great thing. I didn't have any idea what being on TV meant.

I certainly didn't expect I would be on TV. I didn't have a TV then, and I hadn't watched TV since I was kid watching cowboy shows with my brother at home. I had no idea what adult entertainment or talk shows were.

All I knew was David Susskind was having women's liberation on TV. And that was great. We were emerging into the public eye.

When we got to the studio we found out that one of us would be on TV. And so of course we chose Kathie. Shulie was the leader but she wasn't there, and Kathie had become the leader in her absence. We thought she would be the best one to talk about women's liberation on TV, to explain it, to get women to join.

But somehow after we arrived— I guess there were 6 of us, but maybe there were more, there could have been 9—

the producers of the show, or whoever, someone decided they wanted Ros instead of Kathie.

We thought that was because of looks. Ros was tall and blond, with long blond hair, she looked like a model. Whereas Kathie was short with very short hair, she looked like Mia Farrow back then.

We had an instant of outrage about this decision. It seemed against the spirit of women's liberation, that the prettiest one be chosen for the show. Hahaha we had just protested the Miss America Contest.

But basically we didn't care because we were so excited that women's liberation was going to be on the show. And we all clustered around Ros in the make-up room.

Ros said she told them she didn't want to be made-up for the show, but they did it anyway. And we clustered around Ros to give her our full support.

We really did not believe back then that any one woman would be a better spokesman than another for women's liberation.

We were still totally democratic back then and egalitarian. We thought Ros would be perfect. We were just mad that it had been decided on looks. But that mad only lasted an instant. Because we were totally joyed Ros would be on. We would have been totally joyed with any one of us. We just wanted women's liberation on.

We all sat together in the studio. There were benches like at a stadium, 3 tiers of benches. We sat together on the top bench.

There were others in the studio audience because Jacqui was on from NOW, and there were 2 others. And I guess NOW members came to support their President. I remember Jacqui then as a pretty brunette.

I don't remember the other 2 women at all. All our focus was on Ros. We wildly cheered everything she said. Our total focus was supporting Ros.

Back then women's liberation was one. And Ros was the extension of us, up on that stage. And I am sure we booed David Susskind every time he said something we didn't like, which we thought disparages women.

Jacqui said in an email last week (we had never met and met on email last week) that she remembers our group "as being very noisy and that David Susskind had intended to make fun of women's liberation on the show, but hadn't succeeded because the guests were too good."

All I remember is we sat together, rooted for Ros with all our hearts. I don't remember one word Ros said, or any of the others. I just remember cheering Ros wildly after everything she said. We all did. We were a magnificent support group.

And I remember standing around Ros before she went on, in the make-up room, where they also fluffed out her hair, gave her glamorous hair-do, as well as make-up. And Ros being one of us as she sat in the make-up chair. A point on the star which was women's liberation. We were other points. But it was one star, we were a whole.

And then we all walked back downtown to the East Village together in the darkened quieter streets. It was a weekday evening, probably night now. We all walked together, all 6 of us. Carol and Kathie and Ros and me and Lynn Laredo and few others.

We were so happy. We were so content with how it had gone. We were so high and happy from it. We loved each other so much, and felt we had accomplished something glorious for women's liberation.

It was just a quiet contentment, we were all quiet in a way. There had been so much yelling and cheering and wild exuberance all thru the show, this was the quiet aftermath. Of perfect satisfaction at how it had gone, and what we did. It was a total oneness.

Women's liberation at its best was always about a oneness. That was what made it so miraculous, that was its source of joy and peace and its liberation. That we turned into one.

I would say before and after this, during its constructive days, there was always unity.

But the perfect oneness was that evening walking down thru dark Manhattan streets, in perfect peace because we were one. It was simple quiet happiness. And very subtle. But completely fulfilling.

Helen did go to the Miss America protest

I met Helen Kritzler at a women's liberation meeting when I got back from Europe in September 1968. We became best friends that night and have been best friends ever since.

Here is a drawing Helen did of herself in college. (When I met her she was 26 years old)

Helen had a car and knew how to drive. On hot
September afternoons she drove us to Jones Beach

Women's liberationists smoke pot on way to Jones Beach

Email from Pat

After I wrote all the chapters above and fixed the typos I sent it off on email to Bob, and Eddie, and Helen, and Pat. I asked Helen and Pat to add their experience of women's liberation. I got this email from Pat the same day:

I was at the David Susskind Show and so was Helen

Dear Anne,

I was there and so was Helen. Maybe Ruth too, I'll ask her. I remember sitting on the rows of benches and it was kind of dark and Ros was being interviewed. I really don't remember anything else.

What I do remember about that evening is that Helen came home with me. I was living on E. 94th St. and First Ave. in a railroad apt with Matthew. We had lots of rooms— 5 in a row, kitchen w/bathtub, living room on the street, and 3 little rooms in between.

Anyway, that's when I first got to know Helen when she stayed over. In fact, she needed a place to stay that night. I offered and was surprised she would come stay with someone she hardly knew. I'd be too nervous to do something like that. She was leaving the next day I think to go organize the Thanksgiving conference in Chicago.

I think Ruth must have been at David Susskind show because I got into Women's Liberation through Ruth who was invited by Ros (they knew each other from the day care co-op), and I had only been to 1 or 2 meetings.

I didn't go to Miss America because I thought it was "frivolous" (that's the word we used on the left). I wasn't yet convinced re: Women's Liberation. It took me a while. I so regret not going to Miss America.

Love,
Pat

Back in Autumn 1968, Shulie, the artist, draws one of the girls in women's liberation

Drawing by Shulamith Firestone, Autumn 1968.
She drew a friend of ours in my East Village apartment and gave it to me right after she drew it. I have held on to it ever since. I scanned her actual drawing for this book.

After the meetings we all went out to a restaurant together

We were young,
we were merry,
we were in women's liberation

May 15, 2011 Sunday morning Tucson Arizona

The pigeons are in the yard eating the potato chips. The birds are in the tree chirping. It is a garden of eden morning here on the desert, pure paradise.

I am working on so many book projects at once now. Discovering you can publish your self, and you can publish your friends— if you do all the work for formatting it for a paperback book yourself, that Create Space or Lulu will print and bind it for you for free, and post it on Amazon for sale. And because Helen is willing to do the covers for me, front and back cover and spine.

No writer can turn down an opportunity like this. It is God's gift to writers. It costs almost no money at all but the labor is monumental. Fortunately I don't mind monumental labor. I am finding it addictive. I like having projects to work on and don't mind at all that the end is nowhere in sight, that process is everything. Because I am learning so much from the process, so much in so many ways.

However the one project I would like to complete now is the booklet I wrote 3 summers ago about the start of women's liberation.

I wrote it because Helen's big brother Eddie begged me to, and because my dear friend Bob Carneiro wanted me to. And after I did it, I posted it up on a blog so anyone who wanted to read it could click it on. Altho I don't think anyone ever did.

I sent it to Eddie and to Bob on email, it answered all their questions. They got me to write what they wanted me to write. They thought it would interest everyone because it interested them.

Eddie's idea was after I wrote mine, Helen would write hers, her experience of it. And then Pat, Helen's best friend, who was also with us in women's liberation back then, would write hers. And that would make a book we would publish.

But it is 3 years later and Helen and Pat did not write theirs. So it is time for me to put mine out as a booklet.

But as soon as I finished writing it back then, I knew there was something left out that I wanted to include. And that it wouldn't be complete until I did, my section of it anyway, my experience. So now that I am ready to start the project of formatting it for publication, it is time for me to write it. I can not wait any longer.

It was easy for me to write about women's liberation 3 years ago once I got going, because I had a full head of steam, and was reliving it all. I am not sure it is possible to come inside after lying in my backyard watching the birds and drinking coffee, and say "I will write about it now because I told myself to write about it now." But how else can I start.

And at least I have started. I have made the decision to do it now and I am at the machine now trying to do it.

The first meetings at the SCEF office were very small. Perhaps 12 women, maybe a few more. And by my second meeting we were meeting at the SCEF office. By the time I showed up for my first meeting in December 1967 it was the last meeting in each others houses. We didn't meet in January 1968 because our group had a big action in Washington, the Jeanette Rankin Brigade.

And because Carol worked at the SCEF office and had the keys, we met there in February, and we met there thereafter. The room was a huge room. And when the meetings had hundreds of people by September 1968, the huge room accommodated all of them even if we were packed in like sardines then.

But during the first months of 1968 we only grew from 20 to 40 so there was plenty of room.

So it was after the first meeting at SCEF office when there were only 20 of us that we decided to go to the Orchidia, a Ukrainian Italian restaurant in the East Village, just a few blocks from the SCEF office, for coffee and food afterwards.

Meetings I had gone to my whole life. Because of my parents I had been a leftist activist since I was in diapers. Altho of course women's liberation meetings were not like any meeting I had been to. They were so thrilling and such an awakening for me. And so very interesting and very meaningful. They were the actual experience of women's liberation, how I got liberated. They were my liberation.

But I think the experience of going out all together to a restaurant together afterwards for coffee and cake or whatever, was also part of the liberation. It was like Act 2 of women's liberation. The meeting was Act 1. Going out together to the restaurant was Act 2.

The first one at the Orchidia I loved because I had never been to the Orchidia, I didn't even know about it. In February 1968 I had only been out of college for 6 months. I had only been living in my own apartment by myself for 6 months. I was still in the great adventure of discovering what the world was like.

I had been in school my whole life. And had had a college student's life in NYC for the 4 years before. Being a young woman in NYC was still brand new for me. I had never been to a restaurant at night which served alcohol. I had only been to coffee shops in the day for breakfast, lunch, or supper. I went there to eat. Or went with a girl friend so we could have a meal together.

I had never been out at night with girls to be together. I was so thrilled. I felt so grown up and found it so wonderful and interesting and so much fun. It was the start of me loving to eat out. I loved being introduced to this new place and ordering lasagna, that is what the other girls ordered so I did too. And I loved the lasagna.

But what was so wonderful and what made it so memorable was how happy we all were. How much we all loved being together in the restaurant, how close we all were after our meeting, how unified we were.

So it wasn't one bit like social life. I knew all about social life, you go somewhere to look for boys. You go there because you hear boys are there. You go by yourself or with a friend to look for boys. That is your purpose. You are looking for a boyfriend.

This time our purpose was to be together. To enjoy each others company after the meeting. It was like the dessert after the meeting. The meeting was the meat and potatoes of women's liberation, this was the dessert. We were very serious during our meetings. We were intensely purposeful.

The meetings were all about purpose. And we were joined in one purpose, the liberation of all women all over the planet. All of us. To liberate ourselves and all women at the same time. Going to the restaurant afterwards was to relax after the meeting.

We had a totally gay time walking over there. We were so merry. And we had a totally gay and merry time in the restaurant. We were very merry. It was not the strained merriment of social life. None of the strained merriment of parties. This was the real thing. This is what joy is.

The joy was completely real because it sprang up from something completely real, and that was our unity, that we had all joined as one for women's liberation. The joy came because we were all one. Joined in one purpose.

I don't remember anything that got said at that first after-meeting-at-restaurant at Orchidia because I was lost in the glory of my first taste of New York City night life, of being a grown up.

It seemed so sophisticated what I was doing. Having lasagna late at night in an East Village hang-out restaurant with these women I felt so close to and who I had a purpose being with them. We were together in one shared purpose. I felt so at home. Perhaps there were 10 or 12 of us, we moved two tables together.

After that, after the meetings we went to Ratner's on Second Avenue and 7th Street. That is a very fancy Jewish dairy restaurant, and was built at the time of the Yiddish theater. It was huge. And they had a long table which could accommodate all of us. All 20 who had been at the meeting. Or 30 if there were more of us.

Because Ratner's was right next door to the Fillmore East, and it was the time of the rock bands era at the Fillmore East, at another very long table fairly close to us, was the rock band which had just performed or perhaps was getting ready to go back for their midnight show.

They and all the people involved with the band were at the other very long table. They looked like royalty in their extravagant outfits made of velvet. They were rock star royalty at the next table not very far from us.

There were 40 at their table too. Altho we were not interested in them, we were totally interested in ourselves.

We could not have been plainer looking compared to rock star royalty holding court at next table. We were in dungarees and tee shirts and no make up. We probably looked like a flock of sparrows compared to the peacocks at the next table.

We all ordered strawberry short cake or cheese cake and coffee. The rock stars were having supper but we just ordered dessert and coffee. And something very beautiful happened. It's not that the meeting continued, but it was another form of the meeting.

I mean it wasn't small talk or chit-chat which went on. But it wasn't being serious the way we were at meetings. The sense of importance was lifted. The feeling that it mattered wasn't there. Because we were just out for a good time, and were there because we just wanted to continue being together and share each others company, it was pure unity and pure joy.

I don't remember anything we talked about at any of the Ratner's coffee and dessert after the meeting, but I know it was a continuation of women's liberation, just a continuation in joy.

It was so much fun and we all had a great time. And we loved it and it made us very happy. Maybe what was said there doesn't matter, it was the spirit of women's liberation that went on that was everything. Our unity, our joy.

And then it got switched to Mitali's, a Greek coffee shop in the West Village. We were there the longest. Until women's liberation broke up into 3 groups and we never all met again, during the middle of its second year.

I loved Mitali's. I hadn't known about it. I guess Kathie who lived close by showed it to us. I couldn't remember its name when I first wanted to write about going there 3 years ago, but I found on internet something Carol wrote about early women's liberation meetings, and she ended with "and who can forget that delicious hot apple pie at Mitali's." So I guess that is what she ordered. I think I ordered a hamburger and coca cola.

But again we were high and happy and in joy, and

continued to talk about women's liberation topics which interested us. And again I don't remember one word of what got said there, but again I remember the experience and how much I loved it.

And how happy I was and how happy we all were. And then the girls who lived in the East Village all walked home together. And that was totally happy too...

Anne finishes telling her story of women's lib

Post script

I realize now Eddie had a genius idea to envision this book as Anne writes her experience, Helen writes hers, Pat writes hers. We are the only 3 women he knows who were in women's liberation at the start. Helen because she is his sister, and me and Pat because we are two of Helen's best friends so we are friends with Eddie.

But Helen and Pat and I know lots of girls who were in women's liberation with us back then. And if this book falls into their hands, I hope they fulfill Eddie's idea. It is a good idea. I hope Helen does write her experience and Pat writes her experience and any of the other women write theirs.

Because I would love to read it!

Love, Anne

May 17, 2011
Tucson, Arizona

I decide to put in Jimmy's poem

After I wrote my Post Script I began formatting this little booklet for publication. But I was stymied at the first step in the publishing process. In order for it to be a regular book (not stapled or coil binding) I had to have 84 pages.

Anne hits a bump in the road

At first I thought, OK I'll add at the end a chapter from the next book I am publishing about my daily life in Tucson.

Anne shops at Sunflower market

But it didn't work with the rest of this book.

So then I remembered the poem my friend Jimmy wrote about his experiences in the '60s. I am going to publish a book of his poems, I know that poem well. I asked him for permission to include it at end of my booklet on start of women's liberation. And by a miracle he said yes.

The poem is called *Then and Now*. Most of it is his tale about his experiences in the '60s, but some of it takes place in 2005 when he sat down and wrote the poem. For my booklet here I took out everything which occurs in 2005 and just left in his tale of his experience in the '60s.

Because I realize the Sixties was a wave. The women's liberation movement arose with that wave, Jimmy's experiences are part of that wave. I think Jimmy's poem adds to the book because it completes a picture of the times.

Plus I admit I am crazy about the poem. It is so real and interesting.

So this is an extract from his whole narrative. You can read the whole poem in his book of poems **Cracks in the Concrete** by James Goldiner. *(Just published!)*

Note: The poem is one whole, so I kept Jimmy's original number for each stanza. But I took out the stanza under it when he talked about 2005.

By Jim Goldiner

then and now
june '67-june '05

1

*****

2

it's spring now
and it was spring in 1967
when mc namara and congress
                              adjusted the law

so we left
              stewart and me
                              with our dogs
for montreal before
the bureaucracy could get going

nine months later
when our time was up
we left for vancouver
the two of us stewart's wife to be and
of course the dogs

we followed the highway out of montreal
to toronto and down to detroit
to avoid the canadian snow

some minor trouble with immigration
then to morehead minnesota
where the ice flipped the car over 360 degrees
no damage but the tires were shot
then fargo...
                    the next day into montana
the snow started to fall

                        3

                      *****
                        4

around midnight we stopped in livingston
the only place open for miles
it was quiet the snow falling
                            no trucks
just us and one waitress
                        maybe two
we ate and talked
the three of us...and jody

after an hour we left

about five miles out of town
                            the snow stops
stewart and carol and the dogs are asleep
mr tambourine is on the radio

i can hear just for a second
                              the sound of her wave

next thing
                    we're sinking into the shoulder
up to a foot of snow
everyone's awake now
out of the car
                    and lennie the big male dog
takes off after the bark of a dog
across a desolate field

there's nothing to do
nowhere to go...
                    luck again
the highway crew is out and
although they weren't supposed to
they pulled us out

we had taken the wrong road...
                              closed in winter

back in the car
it was uneventful through idaho and
most of washington state

vancouver...
                    a nice city then maybe
you could get out of town into the hills
maybe fifteen minutes
the cops of course
were the same as in most places

stewart and carol left for san francisco
and on a warm beautiful day
lennie and me started driving east
following the border

the farther east
the more the clouds formed
the colder it got
then the snow
and more snow until
we were stopped in trail bc
two days in a blizzard
with singing canaries in the small

                              hotel coffee shop

                    5
                  *****
                    6

when the weather cleared we
passed through the immigration point
at porthill idaho
talked about dogs
with the immigration officer

and the chinese made
flannel shirt i had on

we followed the road to bonners ferry
and sandpoint

                          then to missoula
following the clark fork river

i'm comfortable in the front seat
with my heater
lennie is sprawled out in the back

we stop by the tracks in whithall
                                  and sleep

breakfast in manhattan montana
                                  near the tracks
the cowboys walk in
another old movie set

                          7

i get into livingston at night
check into a motel
and spend the next two days eating in the diner
no sign of jody

finally i ask a waitress
and on my third day in livingston
i have dinner after midnight

we don't say much to each other

on my way out
my stomach slides back down into itself
into a warm blue place

as she hands me the keys
and directions to her apartment

8

*****

9

i bring my things up
along with lennie
                    to the top floor
of a three story house and
it's comfortable there
in small town montana

i can't sleep

at six jody comes home
and we talk for awhile

from the window
we look out to the court house below
the quiet empty streets and
to the snow covered mountains
                                    north of town

it was not your good looks
it was your look
and as complicated
                    or as simple
as the sound of your wave

it's lasted a lifetime

10

we woke that first morning
walked around town
talked to a few people
had breakfast
        walked some more
                and talked

i drove jody to work
had dinner
came home and slept

when jody came home
we talked slept and
driving into the country that afternoon
felt good
we began to settle into each other

the road to yellowstone was closed for the winter

11

i'm here for about a week
everything seems okay or so i think
i talk to the old men
who sit in chairs on main street
who no longer seem interested
in politics or religion
we talk about dogs and

i get along with most
of the younger people
who no longer belong there

a little after midnight
i pick up jody

driving home
i get an odd feeling behind me
suddenly the flashing lights are on
two locals and the highway patrol
and although it may seem trivial now
their attempt at intimidation

                          was not

their top lights whirling

12

i pull over
was i speeding? no
—hello jody
jody says hello
—can i see your license and registration?
—sure was i speeding?
—no
he goes back to the other two cars
and they look at the car
and talk
and look
—you've got till tomorrow morning to get over
to the court house get montana plates on the car

—oh?
—you born in canada or the states?
—new york
—what were you doing in canada?
—i was working in montreal
—can i see your draft card?
—it's at home
—that's illegal you know

> pronounced as if the united
> states were in the middle
> of a world war and
> espionage was everywhere

—yeah but i'm finished with that
and all the while lennie
is barking in the back seat
trying to get out of the window
—you go get your papers
and bring them over to the station house

> all nice and polite

then the highway guy
steps up front
tells me again about the plates

they follow us
i get "the papers" and
follow them back to their house and
into the talk it over room

> just like the movies

they look at the papers
ask a few questions
make a few notes

                              i thought it was a slow night
but it wasn't

then it comes
—where are you living james?
i tell them with jody
—yeah that's the report we got
report? what report to myself
—you married james?
                              all chummy on a first name basis
—no
—jody's not married neither huh james?
—no not that i know of
i sort of hum to myself
—we don't go for that sort of thing around here james
that's a criminal act carries a sentence of five years
and a $500 fine
—i didn't know that
—well now you do see that you act accordingly
—you can go now

they were all too nice and polite
like evil in the movies
the same red lights whirling
outside of the police house and
my stomach is slipping away again
this is not a joyful anticipatory slippage

                              13

                              *****

14

next morning
i don't trust the only lawyer in town

finally in a small corner of missoula
i get advice from a law professor
—they're full of shit kid
but it's a small town
they'll get you if they want

i rent the second floor
we have a duplex
and that's the end of that

15

we talked and talked
ulcers at eighteen
—i wish i were jewish
i think i saw moses on the day i was born

jody grew up in livingston
among the mountains

too gentle against all the snow and wind
from livingston to bozmon then berkeley and flagstaff

—i wish i were jewish

married for three months at seventeen

a few more escapes
then back to livingston
—i had a horse when i was young
and road bareback through the snow

she carried the aura of a slightly
failed innocence…a vulnerability

—i too easily become what others are

it was 1968
it was very easy very comfortable
for both of us

16

after awhile
jody had to stop working
we were both sick

first the doctor blamed jody
then me but
it was his bad medicine
                              sometime earlier

we couldn't get served
in any restaurant in the county
                              not even coffee

17

jody wanted to leave
she had to leave
get away from the people she
had known all her life
go to missoula become anonymous

i couldn't go
not then
there were things i had to do in new york
before i could do anything else

18

i left on a monday
i moved some of jody's things
to the train station

we said good-bye at the post office
it was a little like dying
when that's not at all
                    what you had in mind

i remember giving you a telephone number
that you could always call
you had none to give me

you never called

two three months later

i could find no trace of you

by the time i reached worden
                              150 miles east
the temperature had climbed to eighty

                    19

i look at the maps and
see booneville missouri
i remember eating chili
four years earlier
during a blizzard
and a motel in sweet springs
the pink motel

chicago the lincoln highway
all the way into new york city
thinking of sad jody

you had no number to give
you never called

                    20
                   *****
                    21

on april 17th of 2005
a hot sunny sunday i
called again and still no you

i pulled out the atlas…
                    and there
i never called in 1968
or thirty minutes ago
                    unlisted they said
but there

i hope you're happy
at least comfortable
and no one else has harmed you

at least comfortable
and as anonymous as you want.

My husband Bill draws Skipper sleeping

I met Jimmy in Tompkins Square Park (in the East Village) when we were both walking our dogs. We are both animal lovers. I hope you enjoyed our little book.

I send all my love to all of you and to your animals too. Love, Anne

The end
Tucson, Arizona
June 2, 2011

An open letter to anyone who wants to write or even dreams of doing it

Go for it!
Writing is easy and fun
Here is my experience

In my NYC family, my mom from Rochester was a nurse, but my dad was high school teacher for Board of Education of City of New York, and ditto all his sisters and their husbands. So were all my parents' friends.

When I looked at the Jamaica High School alumnae website, where I went to high school, I discovered all the girls in my classes had become school teachers.

It never crossed my mind I would be anything other than a school teacher too until I walked into my first women's liberation meetings. The dream didn't take hold for me till the second year of women's liberation when the writers joined. They were sent by their editors "to find out what these chicks are up to." And they all stayed and joined it themselves.

That's when I discovered not all girls become school teachers or social workers some become writers. I was amazed that they would dream so high. I had always loved reading, reading and swimming were my two passions as a child. But the idea that I could create books for others to enjoy, to give that pleasure to readers that books gave me, it just never occurred to me to dream that high.

I will always be grateful to women's liberation for putting the idea into my head and giving me examples of others who were doing it.

It has brought me happiness for a lifetime.

So now I want to encourage others to go for it.

There are as many individual paths to becoming a writer as there are individuals. But this is the path which I took.

November is National Write a Novel in a Month and a month before November '08, my friend Lisa in Tucson told me about it, and suggested I do it. But I was used to writing short stories and posting them on my Blog (the stories are mostly about my yesterday)— I never wrote a novel and didn't know how.

So I just wrote polite thank you back to Lisa.

But thank God she pushed me. Because when November 3rd rolled around, I decided to give it a try. And to my big surprise, I loved doing it.

I just went to my machine when I woke up with cup of coffee and pack of cigarettes, and wrote for 45 minutes each morning for 3 straight weeks. I still spent my afternoons and evenings posting on current events forum.

I was doing it for a week when Lisa encouraged me to register at the site (NANO) (it is free) and then I received their pep-talk emails, which they sent out to everyone.

Lisa was doing it too, even tho she had never written in her life, she is a painter.

But this is a great way for anyone who has ever dreamed of being a writer to do it. Every November there is another one. I hope you consider doing it too. All you have to do is write for 45 minutes each day for month of November. No editing! No re-writing!

You can begin by telling about your yesterday too, but

after you have done that several times, start to write a story which is long enough to hold your interest to keep telling it for a while.

(Telling a story means "and then" "and then" "and then." First this happened, then that happened, then that happened, then that happened.)

This will give you experience in narrative (telling a story) and there is very good chance that in the middle you will "find your own voice."

This means right in the middle of telling your story, suddenly you hear a voice in your head dictating a different story.

This one is about your earliest childhood, it is all things you have forgotten, and the voice is different, it is in the first person (even if you have been writing in 3rd person) and it is very personal. And you will love it!

If this happens, immediately stop writing what you were writing, and instead start writing everything you are hearing.

This is called "finding your own voice" as a writer, it makes writing so easy and fun, you just take down what it says— or as they say "you get out of the way, and the story writes itself."

That is the way I became a writer back in NYC. I was in my late 20s then and had just been fired from my job. Bill was working as Wall Street messenger then for $96/week. He said "why don't you become a writer, I will support you." Since I now had the dream of writing, I wanted his great offer. I decided to do it.

So I wrote three tiny 2 page stories about my yesterday and then sat down to write long story, I wrote it in 3rd person and it was about a love affair before I met my husband. That topic interested me enough to keep telling the story.

But right in the middle of it, I was a few weeks into it, I heard that voice dictating a whole other story. It was my littlest little girl experiences.

It is the same as learning how to balance on a bicycle. One day they are supporting you, and you are pedaling, and then suddenly out of nowhere, you balance. You can ride a bike.

You never thought it would happen to you, even tho you watched all your friends do it, because it looks like magic.

It is the same way with writing. You push yourself along telling a story, and then suddenly you balance. You hear that voice and simply take down what it says. The story writes itself, you get out of the way.

But you can only learn how to balance on a bike when you are on a bike, and you can only hear your own voice, while you are at the machine writing. But it is as natural and effortless as learning how to balance on a bike. It comes to all.

Guess what! CreateSpace owned by Amazon publishes any book written by anyone for free, but you have to do all the work yourself. No one even reads it.

You have to format it for a paperback book, all they do is press a button to print and bind it, and post it for sale on Amazon.

When I saw the technical work involved in formatting my novel into a paperback book I was terrified. I didn't even know what they were talking about or how to do any of it.

But I was too deep into it to quit. I wanted to publish my novel now, I didn't just want it lost on my computer.

It turns out CreateSpace has community boards. And there are angels on it (people who have published lots and lots of books, are completely experienced) and they walk us newbies thru everything. Ones even less experienced than me, they wrote their book and don't even know how to indent a paragraph or what a tab is or how to edit.

It turned out everything which seemed impossibly hard when I first heard about it, is not hard, you just press a button in your word processing program.

But of course I needed to learn from the community boards which button? where? things like that. They have the patience of saints there and love to help.

I tell you all this because it is God's gift to writers. That we can publish ourselves. CreateSpace also does videos, and music, photography books, art books, comic books.

Lulu does this too. It was first started by Lulu.com. Everyone at CreateSpace started there. Both places are wonderful and many publish at both places. Both Lulu and CreateSpace are free, they publish your book for free and post it on Amazon. A gift from Heaven to all artists.

I tell you all this to encourage you to go for it! If I could do it anyone can. Before I began writing I was convinced I didn't have a creative bone in my body.

I had always loved writing book reports and compositions for school, and always loved writing letters. But I was never artistic in anyway.

Because it turns out it is all there under the surface for

everyone. But you have to be willing to give it a whirl for it to emerge. There is no such thing as talent. It is only when you are actually doing it, that interesting and surprising things happen.

Writing is a big treat you give yourself, because it is way to get to know yourself.

It is never too late to start. Whenever you do is the perfect time. And there is nothing to compare with the freshness of your early beginning.

So think of starting writing, as like the beginning of Spring. Later you will develop more skills, but there is nothing like the beginning. When all the miracles, freshness and inspiration happen.

I wish you luck on your enterprise!

I love you,

Anne

For cartoonists, painters, photographers, musicians, movie makers, all artists

What Lulu and Create Space does for us writer, they do for you too. If you do the work yourself they will produce it and sell it on Amazon, all for free. It is God's gift to artists that we can share our work with the world.

Other Books by Anne Wilensky

Haiku Helen Press is Helen Kritzler and Anne Pyne
I do the books Helen does the covers

Novels

Ruthie Has a New Love, a novel
Published 2009

Girl Blog From Tucson, a novel of sorts
published   2009

MORE Girl Blog From Tucson
Published 2010

History

Not what you'd expect
    How the women's liberation movement
    started
    My personal experience of it
    Published June 26, 2011

And my new book is just published

Sweet Sound of Bird Song

written by Anne Wilensky with cartoons by Billy Stampone

About the year 2010-2011 in my life

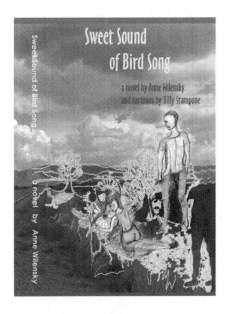

Thank you Jimmy for being a lovely friend and for letting me excerpt your poem in this book.

Thank you Helen for helping me with my books and giving me such beautiful covers.

Jimmy's book of poems is just published now too

It has the whole of the poem I excerpted in this book, and his other wonderful poems.

Cracks in the Concrete by James Goldiner

All books by Anne Wilensky or Jim Goldiner can be ordered at Amazon.com and at any on line bookseller.

Or ask your local bookstore

Create Space lets its authors offer a discount to all readers.

For 40% off on this little womens lib book

Go to **www.createspace.com/3617012**
And enter Discount Code **K8Y8QVRA** at check out

*Lifeguard Jill chatting with Anne in water at Tucson
public pool*

For all

*I send you our beautiful Arizona sunshine, our flawless blue
skies, and the sweet clarity of our birdsong
Let every day come up roses for you
Love, Anne*

46754566R00060

Made in the USA
Charleston, SC
24 September 2015